PINE TREE

Life Cycles

Jason Cooper

Rourke
Publishing LLC
Vero Beach, Florida 32964

www.rourkepublishing.com

PHOTO CREDITS: All photos © Lynn M. Stone except pp. 10, 22 (stage 1) © Breck P. Kent

Editor: Frank Sloan

Cover and page design by Nicola Stratford

Library of Congress Cataloging-in-Publication Data

Cooper, Jason, 1942-
  Pine tree / by Jason Cooper.
      p. cm. -- (Life cycles)
Summary: Describes the life cycle of the pine tree and explains why pine forests are important to humans, animals, and other plants.
Includes bibliographical references and index.
  ISBN 1-58952-706-2 (hardcover)
  1. Pine--Life cycles--Juvenile literature. [1. Pine. 2. Trees.] I.
Title. II. Series: Cooper, Jason, 1942-   Life cycles.
  QK494.5.P66C66 2003
  585'.2--dc21
                                2003011551

Printed in the USA

CG/CG

Table of Contents

About 45 kinds of pine trees grow in the United States.

The Pine Tree

Everyone knows the pine tree with its long, green, needle-like leaves. None of the needle-leaved trees lives across a greater area than the pines. Pines of one kind or another grow from the Arctic Circle south to Guatemala, North Africa, and the islands of Malaysia. Scientists know of about 100 **species** of pines. Mexico has the most species, about 60.

A few of the pines are short and twisted. But most pines are tall trees with straight trunks.

This forest of pines in north Florida is at the edge of a salt marsh, close to the Gulf of Mexico.

Pines are usually tall and straight, like these in south Florida.

Some grow to a height of almost 200 feet (61 meters). Even the largest pine, though, begins life as a tiny seed.

The seeds of this open Jeffrey pine cone in California
have been shed.

Pine Seeds

In pine trees, the little seeds develop in pine cones. You can usually find open pine cones lying at the base of pine trees. Most of these old, open cones have already shed their seeds.

Some pine concs are quite large. A California sugar pine cone may be 30 inches (76 centimeters) long!

This is the male pollen cone of a pinyon pine in Arizona.

Pine trees have male cones and female cones on the same tree. Male cones produce tiny grains of dust-like **pollen**. Wind blows pollen into the air and onto the female cones. Seeds develop from the mixture of pollen and eggs within the female cone.

After the seeds ripen, the cone opens and sheds its seeds. The seeds of most pine species have wing-like parts. The "wing" shape allows them to float a greater distance from the parent tree.

Pine seeds don't do well in shade. Seeds falling directly under a parent tree are less likely to begin growing, or **germinate**.

Pine seeds develop inside a closed cone.

Many kinds of pines have seeds with a "wing."

Pine seeds float to earth. Sunshine, water, and air help them germinate. A tiny root breaks through the seed's shell. The root soaks up water and gains a hold in the soil.

A pine seedling grows up through a forest floor in New Hampshire.

Seed To Tree

The new tree is called a seedling. At first it lives on food stored in the seed.

As the roots branch downward, the seedling reaches upward. It soon sprouts leaves. The main job of the leaves is to make food for the tree. The leaves use sunlight to make food sugar in a process called **photosynthesis**.

Meanwhile, the tree's roots grow larger, too. They anchor the tree and soak up water and **nutrients**.

Pines can survive fire that isn't too hot. This fire, however, burned hot enough to kill several pines.

The pine grows taller and thicker over time. It may live to be 100 years old. Some of the bristle cone pines of the American west, however, have lived more than 4,500 years! They are among the oldest land plants in the world.

Most pines eventually die from disease, wind damage, or fire. Their old trunks rot away. They are still useful, however. Their nutrients are recycled by nature into the soil. Some of those nutrients may very well find their way into a new pine seedling!

Pine Forests

Pine trees are at their finest in natural forests. Some of the largest pine forests are in Western mountains and in the sandy soil of the Southeast.

Ponderosa pines stand tall in a Colorado mountain forest.

Pine cones lie on a blanket of old pine needles.

Pine forests have a carpet of brown pine needles. These are needles that have died and fallen from the trees. Most pine needles live for three or four years before being shed. Healthy pines never shed all their needles at the same time.

The marten lives in pine forests where it hunts pine squirrels.

Natural pine forests are important to a variety of other plants and to several kinds of animals. Squirrels and seed-eating birds, for example, eat pine seeds. Pine **martens**, searching for squirrels, live among the pine branches.

Pines are also of great value to humans. They yield timber for building and sticky **resin** for many products, including turpentine. The pine is certainly one of North America's great natural treasures.

Stage 1:
These male
pollen cones make
powdery pollen

Stage 2:
Pollen unites with
female pine parts
to form a seed

Stage 3:
A pine seedling sprouts
from a tiny pine seed

Stage 4:
Pine seedlings grow into
large, adult
pine trees

Glossary

germinate (JUR muh NAYT) — to begin to grow from a seed; the beginning of plant growth

martens (MART unz) — tree-climbing members of the weasel family

nutrients (NEW tree entz) — things that when taken into a plant are good for it, such as certain minerals in the earth

photosynthesis (foh toh SIN thuh sess) — the process by which green plants change sunlight into food for themselves

pollen (POLL un) — dust-like grains made by flowers to help make new flowers

resin (REZ un) — a sticky substance found in pine trees and used to make turpentine and other products

species (SPEE sheez) — within a closely related group of plants or animals, one certain kind, such as a ponderosa pine

Index

Further Reading

Fowler, Allan. *Pine Trees.* Children's Press, 2001

Freeman, Marcia S., and Gail Saunders-Smith. *Pine Trees.*
    Pebble Books, 1999

Parker, Edward. *Trees and Plants.* Raintree, 2002

Websites to Visit

http://dixiesd.marin.k12.ca.us/dixieschool/Pages/naturetrail/pines/pine2.html

http://www.yahooligans.com/Science_and_Nature/Living_Things/Biology/Botany/Types_of_Plants/Trees/

About the Author

Jason Cooper has written several children's books about a variety of topics for Rourke Publishing, including the recent series *Life Cycles* and *Fighting Forces.* Cooper travels widely to gather information for his books.